I am safe as I am

Sadey Dong

Presentation by *BookLeaf Publishing*

Web: www.bookleafpub.com

E-mail: info@bookleafpub.com

ISBN:9789358318395

First edition 2024

DEDICATION

I would like to thank my friends and family who were always supportive during this journey. I am grateful also to all the help given from my professors, especially professor Stephanie Anderson: I would never be able to write so much poetry if not for your classes!

PREFACE

On a court made of words,
Time is my only verdict.

safe as I am

The trees are melting into forests
Looming street lamps over you branches
reaching
you unseeing the people watching you didn't
notice

And there's fire roaring in the distance
Fire you are not aware that you'd set

The sky is looming over you over-
hear people say "It's pressing down"
They flee and cast sideways glances at you
They flee and the trees melt into oil paint.

They say that's how you remember things
With your back to thin branches of melting trees
When you close the door behind
the day it officially ends

When you keep it open there would be thieves.
Sometimes you hear the wind whisper when you
are deep in thought

Thinking but it is not only you in longing
The trees are the thieves are the ghosts of the
dead

And please come home, the ticks of the clock
are bothering me they are ticking
Ticking ticking way too quickly

Am I losing track of time now
am I forgetting who you are
Are the colors melting dripping onto my
precious carpet
The one I bought when you weren't here yet
The pills the pills all the ones you made me take
are choking me

Before saving me from an ultimate death
I wish I'd have known you for someone else
I wish you were mine and I was your someone
else
The fire in the fireplace crackle vibrant and alive
You blurring by the clock...

What if the place you felt at home in is never
home to me, mother?
Your back hunched over your hands red running
through ice cold water
our faucet just never works properly
the colors of our furniture never a symphony

I never knew how so many discordant colors
could melt into bleach mother

I'm wearing myself out mother I'm oscillating
between thoughts mother
I miss you but I don't how could you fade
into memory when you are still there
Just thousands of miles away from me mother
And of course I didn't say this to you
of course I wouldn't say any of this to you
Because this is my way of remembering
My colors faded into words, mother.

I'm heading down the slope now
Invisible people are chasing after me
The trees the thieves the ghosts of the dead
I am safe as I am mother I am safe as I am.

Breaking, Old Hours

The hands of the clock hesitant
Like a ferris wheel suspended.
They lived that ride to the full
Fearful yet excited at its peak.

He said he'd squeezed through the window
To get onto that train,
And slept on the floor under a row of seats.
The aisle was another window, just for him,
At a time when all he sees
Was other people's feet.

That second hand TV was always blinking
It's eyes unseen, unseeing.
Light reflected off the four walls
Of that tube shaped apartment you call
Home,
That latent distance made you
Succumb to visibility.
Now you are nonentities
In China's best ant colony
They call Beijing.

A few summers before you had me
You've both gotten used to dreaming
Mosquito disturbed, sweat soaked dreams

About a gold rush not so prosperous.
Disappointed idealism drowned in drips
From the leaking faucet you couldn't
Afford to fix.

Now is not the nineties
We still tear up, we still repeat
The old hours that circle back
Till the clock stopped moving
And we moved--
To a slightly bigger apartment
Still in Beijing.

lost in translation

How do you translate your love for me?

Sacrifice.

What you don't know is
With everything there comes a price.

The price of sacrifice is that
Everything you sacrificed
Eventually weighs on me.

I'm Atlas lifting up the sky.

How do you translate care?

Curses and cries.

You echo even when I'm away.
You echo inside me.
You echo me hollow.

I'm a translation of you, you make up
My semi-autobiographical.

the branches are loaded

The branches are loaded with flowers
The way guns are with bullets.
They can't tell between late spring
And early autumn.
Cherry blossoms killed many men.

Weeds hug the shore.
They may be the reason, I thought,
She never lets me too near
The water. Or is it because
She herself can't swim
That she sent me to learn swimming.

She is afraid of many things,
And there are many more she never thought of
trying.
She is so used to doing what she should do--
That time became used to it too,
And passes her by.

She is timeless, misinterpretation,
Nothing but (   )
Something else.
She is the moon who
Allowed me to become a planet.
She is my identity

Reasons why I was led
To sit under Osmanthus trees.
She gave in and held me,
Months later
I finally saw conformity.

She took me to foreign places
Many of which I don't even remember.
Youth is not to be cherished
But to be spent skipping
Across puddles, jumping
Into them, and--
Splatter.

Ink smeared on plain paper.
She tries to pull me back.
Her gravity internal, forceful...
I swam too far I drifted out of orbit.

Let me pull you into the water this time.
Roll up the bottom of your trousers.
Don't worry about your glasses,
Or our cats, or my father.

Let me take you somewhere we can
Be younger
Before any human voices wake us:
It's autumn again.

The trees are saturated with color
Red and yellow.
The many shades we could rest under
Dry and cold.

I still like to hide under
Smooth white surfaces,
To stand tall at the edges
Of beds, and reach for your hands,
To crawl across the living-
Room, with a book in my mouth,
To speak: "   ".

Squirrels swam across grasses, branches,
Odysseus is still traveling--
Osmanthus flowers are killing many me.

Beijing, 2010, Inner Mongolia

It's hard to imagine a cactus underwater
Prosperity an illusion to hold onto,
    oldness somewhere to escape to
For drought is a season
    only so many people knew
And smears and splatters is how
    I'll write about you

My youthful vitality seemed to come
    at the cost of your absence
You returned to the place I love
    only because of you
So far North
    I lost sight of you
Excessive expression losing hearing
Silent afternoons the cold sun on colder tiles
I'm fluent in two languages
    Yet I don't know
    how to talk to you.

You could still stand just one night before
And now you sit at the dining table
With your head down low
    My head down low.
    I can't look at you
When you are trying to make yourself small.

Would making yourself small make you young
again too?

In May you're a new man.
And September was always the best season
Of barren slopes to run up of, wastelands
To walk out of the train station, see you waiting

There.

Head Above Water

I ascend the flight of stairs and see you waiting
    at the end
Of the dim hallway and you walk toward me
Two years a sentence encased in a wooden
    cabinet
we couldn't afford. You cover my eyes and hand
    me a ruler
I cut up / the sentence / we pretend not to hear
Syllables slip through our fingers / screaming.

Your curtains flutter / my diary weighed down
By broken verses / drifting numbers
When your hair was gray / our days
were soaked in cold water / I fled on tiptoes
From crowds / through crowds / to get to you

/

You talk to me the way my cat worries her
    worries
I don't care if she's smart or if she loves me I
    just want her to be happy
But she doesn't look happy at all she's always
    slumped on her desk
I worry about her for nights on end

You were absent I wonder where you've been

how you've been doing
It's April you return you look happier you look
        South others look
Down at their notebooks they count the numbers
        you count the days
And I don't feel the gale winds or fugitive youth
        I can only feel
You drifting somewhere you'd feel happier
        closer to some person younger
/

In summer I became you pretending to outgrow
        ten years
Christmas an advance / you left behind paying
        debt
Before even buying cars and apartments / you
        crumple brow furrowed
A cup too full you overflow.
Money choices anxiety responsibility /// "it's too
        late now get some sleep"

I planned train tickets for you / wrote lines you'd
        never read between
To see meaning come through / you became
light
        enough to float off my pages
To get drunk and sing into beer bottles / read
        otherwise unintelligible verses
I developed a preference for old paper / you

fresh like Beijing's summers
Especially the first half last year / because I
wasn't there and you weren't there.

why is the world full of mirrors?

Why is the world full of mirrors?
The last flames of hell died to ashes
After breakfast / Es ist zu kalt heute.
When I was her age / I still see images
I still hear you / constantly / viciously
Dare to think / hands in pockets
Above the sound of waves crushing to shore.
You let me tear up / get some sleep
And I waded into the water.
There would be times I remember myself
Strands to pieces / a tiny shadow
Singing on buses. I close my eyes
And agreed that the water was more
Departure than the sand.

Them Times

It was there one moment
And then it was not
Water
Was something that happened.

It is okay to not go to sea world
To outgrow it
Even breaking into it at night
But not the city

It has so many theme parks
It became one
A crowd of icons
Too clamorous for poetry

Freedom=road trips
Might only be valid at eighteen
Or if you are one of the beats
That has a pen pal auntie.

Oh Allen, Allen
If only you'd lived
In black mountains, wooden cottages
Among smoky trees.

You'd see

Frosted windows, frozen locks of hair
Despite countless experiments
Of ecstasy.

Oh all the times you got drunk
Hanging out with delinquent crowds
Things didn't come full circle
Only because the world isn't one.

You must allow for pens to not
Be as decisive as typewriters
And for poetry to flow sometimes
Like creeks that suspend breathing.

It's always them times
That put Lucien Carr behind bars
Them times them times them times them times
them times them times them times
That took down banners on bridges overnight.

Oh but freedom is too much
For them times to bear
So we hopped aboard jet-lag
As a getaway carrier.

I am on fire, or is the world

Out of focus. Heartbeats are
way too conscious.
Thumps   on my eardrums
I am on fire
Or is the world.

Portable typewriters tap--
Dancing to Jazz
Their manic rhythm
Under water, sound travels
In bubbles, scatters because

Of bubbles.
Helicopter blades sliced
Up, my dreams
Blank letters levitated
In bubble wrap

The possibility of reaching   out
To reality, another sanctuary,
Of following suit, with nothing
To follow, of coughing insides out
Despite perfect health.

Noise

historic times

sound like noise

There is no such thing

As   "for your benefit"

BOURGEOUIS
PLEASURE

To wealth, not ourselves

I didn't get anything
You worshiped
Wrong.

bring our complaints
offer insincere praise
To: past spectres
potent silhouettes
even worse
sacrifice words
To
indents, time to rhyme
U / U / U / U / U /
constraints of meters are about to end.

they keep saying

They keep saying transparency is not enough.
They said we need perfect timing.
Six to eight in the morning. Not a second later
than that.
They set their gaze on each and every one of us
Slowly moving in line.

They said we need something stronger than tape.
They sealed windows shut. Put iron bars on
doors.
They said they are sorry for the thirty people that
died in the fire.

They said we need to eliminate all possibilities.
They pulled people out from their homes
Put them in places they call hospitals.
They beat the corgi until it lay limp on the
sidewalk.

They put on their uniforms.
They took off themselves.

what is symmetrical?

21

Everything is symmetrical.
What do you want?
In silence, his eyes open.
They make me up
When there's light I see out.
When night falls I see me.
And imprisons me.
Cells.
The guy next door sits on his bed
What is symmetrical?

21st Century Chinese Moloch

Future brings freedom! Future brings success!
Future is the new Chinese gospel!
Hail Future!
Kneel, before the altar!
Present, infants with the name of Present!
They watch, in utter fascination, how Future
dips the infants, head down, into different kinds
of sauce!
Red sauce time, green sauce endurance, yellow
sauce hope...
Future devours them all! Future feeds on the
specters of youth! Future devours, spitting out
skeletons, skeletons the embers of life! Future
burps, greedy, longing for more!

Future is the new generation!
Future is best loved among their children!
Future Orients! Future rules!
Future is the cult of the century!
Future why people still go to work when they
are fifty!
Future why couples endure each other and not
divorce!
Everything is done for Future!

LONGER

working hours!
MORE
income!
BETTER
education!
MORE
income!
LONGER
working hours!

Future the luxury of the poor, the damned!
Future is all they have, all they dream of!
Future swindles! Future deceives!
Future the expectant gaze of clear, desperate
eyes!
Future the unwavering, pitiful gaze of the
hopeful!
Future who close his own eyes and stays blind!

Future whose women are chained down by iron
shackles!
Future in whom sexism is the new imperialism!
Future who won't recognize crowds, won't see
pieces of plain, white paper!
Future who erases voices, who takes down street
plates, who puts people behind bars!

ERROR. The page you are trying to visit does not exist.

Future who plays with numbers, and when it all
went wrong sends people into high fevers!
Future who never sealed doors, who managed to
save all people from fires!
Future who never admits bad decisions were
made, but tries to cover it up with others!

Future in whom there's never school bullying!
Future who is very friendly to the queer
community!
Future in whom everyone is equal!
Future who will shatter hierarchy!
Future whose teenagers commit suicide only
because of their own problems!
Oh wait, Future's teenagers never commit
suicide!
Everybody lives a hundred years old and dies of
oldness!

(would Future die of oldness?)

Future the naughty child who is always
forgiven!
Future who disappoints and never apologizes!
Future, who, after all this time, you and I still
have faith in!

to remember

That scarlet silence
Of red roses
Lying on green lawns

A naked reminder
That we evolve around:
A center.

The camera lens
Flashing red, indignant
Its massive cyclops body
Hidden--

It is the eye that allows us to remember.

reverse

It's all way more natural once you
Remove your eyes from your feet,
And look into the eyes of another
One they'd refer to as
The inevitable other.

If an inevitable is founded on
Ends instead of the whole spectrum
What identifies as the inevitable
Would actually look backward
And blinded.

If the inevitable is concrete only in
An individual, it would be wrong
To turn blind to the individual
Even if the individual is
A woman

Who can't escape history,
Who never displayed autonomy,
(really?)
An addition attempting
To be core.

Color the black canvas
With words,

The ill sighted sees redemption
A reverse of
Reification.

A Void

Regression is progression
In the numerable
Infinity of masses

Now is not a time
Of vacancy, incomplete theories
Quiet grass lawns in universities
Morality took the form of mobility
Music blaring through truck windows on
highways
Singing all colors are beautiful, aren't they
Rainbow colors, and yellow brown and black.

This conversation is too dry
We stare at each other's faces
Believing a void is what communicates
The untranslatable. For years.
So we split into even more masses
Despite favoring fireworks over explosives.

The aftershock of the earthquake shattered vases
That once held poppies
Blown over from Flanders fields
Pools glistening dark, glass shards, wounded
Petals. Silence too dense for breathing.
Cult is our most valuable heritage--

Because we lost track of money.

Salt Burns

31

Salt burns,
Heals.
We are many
Cycles.
Plurality is tenderer
When speaking
Foreign
Tongues.

No One Saw Us That Evening
Hand in Hand

The hours we stole

                    Shorter...

with every breath we took,
Till age cannot be taken advantage of anymore.
We were never reckless,

                      ever longing,

But I had desperately wished that you would
       grant my wishes the way you solved my
problems.

I saw your rejection and I saw your reaction,
you ascended that flight of stairs you thought it
       was heaven.
Secrets weighed me down
Love's echo echoed on......

If I wish to exit I must
sprint

                           away

spill liquor at every harbour,
spend my mornings warped in hangover,
       and elegize you
Infinitely, over and over

                 in our finite years.

How the Day Died

if one sees / by correction
conceive of places / as outlaws
one could multiply / the confession
obscurity / no longer
the most ordinary / penalty
no more / enduring
than a warm americano
on a sunday evening
never as / silent
as airport lounges
at three in the morning

he said *Raleigh was right*
one hand pushing his suitcase
left you in LA

The day died at dusk.

You both believe in high risk
High return, spend money like water
Breathe triumph like air
But money is low stake
Love is high.
How pathetic is detouring around
The gigantic bubbling swamp
And coming full

circle?

One step forward and three steps back.

You sat at the bar after the day died
Watching them talk
She showing him your engagement rings
The expression on his face hidden
You sat back on the sofa
Watching candle wicks dance.
You didn't know October died
Just for him.

What are places but traces of the past?
He was constantly on the move,
Nights spent flying more than those spent
Sleeping in his own bed.

What is obscurity but mutual negation?
He took down walls
Of poems he'd wrote for you
Finally looking

Through his bedroom window.

What are Americanos, Sunday evenings, airport
lounges, three a.m.s in the morning?
Dead Octobers.
The air turns cold, the leaves gold.

And there will be curtains of stars, moon
eclipses
Northern lights, polar nights
But when the day died
He took away the night.

what are you thinking?

"Look at the fire, and tell me,
Were you happy? In the city."
I meet the gaze of your grandfather,
An older you
You won't grow into.

The war is over now.
What are you thinking?
White butterflies, 30,000 of them,
In the creeks, in the sea, in ruins, asleep.
Autumn here is way too naughty,
I almost lost you in
The margins of
The city.

I'm drawing stamens on your scar.
What are you thinking?
Our teenage years blossom,
Perpetually hungry for soil,
Thirsty for rain.
We were two trees with feet.

The black bear escaped into someone's home.
What are you thinking?
A bomb yet to explode, shivering
Under the kitchen table.

They went after it with spears and lances.
It died. You were the spears and I was the
lances.

The aerial defense alarm went off again.
Where are you?
A woman in red waltzing along it.
What are you thinking?
You held the massive painting on your head,
running.
Do you hear the planes coming?

I raced for three hours to pick corn poppies for
you.
What are you thinking?
I stuffed petals between your lips.
They spill, scarlet against your dark skin.
The sky wept blood, seeping
Into dark, charred earth.

It's 7 a.m. now, *what are you thinking?*
It's afternoon now, *what are you thinking?*
It's midnight now, *what are you thinking?*
I watch as the fire dances barefoot.
What are you thinking?